The Book of Levinson

poems by

Cat Dixon

Finishing Line Press
Georgetown, Kentucky

The Book of Levinson

ACKNOWLEDGMENTS

"Haunted House—October 2014" *Linden Avenue Literary Journal*. July 2016.
"I First Heard Your Name on the Radio" *Linden Avenue Literary Journal*. July
2016.
"Leaving Maryam Sorinet Hotel" *Gravel Magazine*. December 2015.
"Pink Shirts" *Gravel Magazine*. December 2015.
"Tremor" *Gravel Magazine*. December 2015.

I am grateful to Bob's daughter, Stephanie Curry, who was gracious enough to
read the poems and answer questions. Thank you.

To learn more about Bob Levinson and his family's work to have him brought
home, please visit: www.helpboblevinson.com.

Publisher: Leah Maines

Editor: Christen Kincaid

Cover Art: Jan Wilson

Author Photo: Jan Wilson

Cover Design: Elizabeth Maines

Printed in the USA on acid-free paper.
Order online: www.finishinglinepress.com
            also available on amazon.com

Author inquiries and mail orders:
Finishing Line Press
P. O. Box 1626
Georgetown, Kentucky 40324
U. S. A.

Table of Contents

*   These poems are based are on signs that Bob Levinson held up in photographs that were sent to his family in 2011. See: http://wapo.st/17Ozdvr

About Bob Levinson

Bob Levinson was taken hostage on March 9, 2007 as he headed to the airport on the Iranian island of Kish. This husband, father of seven, and retired FBI agent vanished after checking out of his hotel. It was reported that Levinson visited Kish Island to investigate a cigarette smuggling case and he was not working for the United States government, but years later in winter 2013, the Associated Press reported that Levinson traveled to Iran because he was under contract with the CIA. It is still not clear to the public what Levinson's role was in Iran, but the last contact from him is an email he sent to a close friend, Ira Silverman, retired NBC investigative producer, asking him if it was a good idea to spend the night on Kish Island.

Just a few months after his capture, Christine Levinson, Bob's wife, traveled to Iran with her oldest son. She pleaded on Iranian news programs for information about her husband, sent letters to the Iranian president asking for help, and along with her children, created a website and a Facebook page to help find Bob. The Levinson family feared they would never see Bob again, but in late 2010 they received a video from Bob's capturers. This short clip of Bob offered them hope and a year later they released the video to the media. In 2011 photographs were sent to the family showing Bob in an orange jumpsuit holding up signs.

The Levinson family does not know who captured Bob. The United States government is now offering $5 million dollars for information leading to his return. No group has taken responsibility for holding Bob and Iran has issued several statements saying the government has no information about his whereabouts. No actual demands for Bob's release have been made to the United States or to the Levinson family. So they wait.

As I worked on these poems, I reached out to the Levinson family and researched hostage situations in the Middle East. I wrote these poems for Bob as he is now without a voice. Bob's family, friends and I want him returned home.

Abduction

"The family of Levinson, a retired FBI agent, has been anxiously waiting for news, any news, about his fate since he vanished during a business trip to Iran in March 2007."
                    —Susan Candiotti, CNN National Correspondent

Last Email

I only want to stay the day.
Fly back to Dubai.
Ira, should I spend the night?
I'm taking the earliest flight.
Thursday I fly into k.
Ira, should I spend the night?
I will do so if needed—
off today for that place.
I'd feel better spending
as little time there as I have to.
Best wishes to you.
Ira, should I spend the night?

Kish Island

The water is so clear
that fish can be seen
swimming all year.
The palm trees planted
in such round bushes
in such perfect formations,
you know this land is rigid
in more ways than one.
The air is so humid and sweet
with flowers, pink in bloom,
your chest tightens,
your eyes water,
your nostrils twitch.

Leaving Maryam Sorinet Hotel

Exhausted, I dragged my suitcase to the curb outside the hotel.
One night. The white palace exterior.
I did not sleep; instead, I thought of home.

When I flung the taxi door open, I didn't look the driver in the eye.
The ride to the airport would take only five minutes;
instead, the roundabout and then the pier.

The airport's the other way,
I choked. Then I awoke
in a windowless room.

I searched my pockets—wallet and cell phone, gone.
My signature on the hotel bill
the only note I left behind.

Tremor

I can't stop trembling.

        I clench my jaw, my fists.

        The men believe it's a tremor and insist I must be older

—my paperwork lies. Tectonic plates slip

        and collide inside my chest. I need to appear calm,

            but the aftershocks give me away.

I drip sweat.

The fault ruptures.

May 11th 2007—33rd Wedding Anniversary

Certain the questions would end,
I planned on being home today—free.
Beg them to follow every lead.
I'm not where I'm supposed to be.
33 years ago I gave you a key
during a few moments of privacy,
and asked you to stay with me.
That key unlocks a room secretly
hidden under our wedding canopy.
Go there now, tear up the ground. See
the shards of glass, find the memory.

A Light Bulb Hangs

A light bulb hangs
from a string
and with every
slam of the door
it swings. Imagine
a body on the gallows,
those last steps, that final blink,
the neck crack.

Hostage

"I have been held here for three and half years. I am not in very good health. I am running very quickly out of diabetes medicine. I have been treated well. I need the help of the United States government to answer the requests of the group that has held me for three and half years. And please help me get home. Thirty-three years of service to the United States deserves something. Please help me."

—Bob Levinson, from a video sent to his family in 2010
https://www.youtube.com/watch?v=knjx0E2xLc0

Orange

I never wore orange—
the color of carrots,
traffic cones,
life jackets,
prison uniforms.
I prefer blue or gray—
muted tones don't call
attention. Gray says
I'm Bob. A regular guy.
Now leave me alone.

WHY YOU CAN NOT HELP ME

I hold up signs in broken English.
They ask if they're right. I nod yes.
No reason to correct their grammar.
The distress signal will not be answered.

. . . — — — . . .

The transmission, static.
The operator, blind and deaf.
The flash, bright.

4 TH YEAR… You Cant or you don't want…?

Maybe they can't.
    Maybe they don't
                want.

Maybe they forgot my name.
When I blink
 I see my name
flash on the back of my eyelids.
I remind myself that is my name.

     I can.
         I want.

The blood thunders in my ears
and the flow of tears has ceased.

     Anne, you can't?

         Anne, you don't want?*

Leave me here planted in dark mud
and muck to find the light. I bloom.

*Anne Jablonski is the CIA analyst who approved the contract
for Levinson's work in Iran. She was fired from the CIA and now
works as a yoga instructor. Her yoga blog inspired parts of this
poem: http://www.yogasetfree.com/foxhole-yoga.html

THIS IS THE RESULT OF 30 YEARS SERVING FOR   USA

What is your name?

    How do you spell it?

Who do you work for?

    Who pays you?

Why are you here?

    Where are you going?

Who knows you are here?

    Who knows you?

How old are you?

    What state you live in?

How many times you traveled here?

    What is your flight number?

What do you know?

    What is your alias?

Did your government send you?

    Where is your country now?

Code

Who was the person that was with you when you called me on the telephone to ask me to marry you?*

Years ago, I had you memorize this question.
Ask me this, I said, *if I am ever captured. Ask me this.*

Did you remember?

I have no way to tell you:

Nadie Horowitz

> N, for north
>
> A, for Ardabil
>
> D, dome
>
> I, Iran
>
> E, earthquake

The last name, coordinates.

The first name means no one in Spanish

**Christine Levinson asked this question while being interviewed on Voice of America in Iran on July 14, 2008. She is still waiting for an answer. See*: https://www.youtube.com/watch?v=ac8giLv1csg

Gout

My wrists swell. The skin splits. The blisters burn at the bone. One night a man slips me vitamin C capsules when no one is around and he tells me his father suffered with his feet. I take the pills, no longer afraid of poison. He asks for nothing in return except my silence as he whispers in broken English his story—too young to say no, too poor to find a way out, too guilty to walk away. Weeks pass before he smuggles in pain medication and news. My family is asking for me, offering a reward, talking to the president. He says it won't be much longer. His pity-filled brown eyes glisten when he tells me his father and mother are both dead. *I have seven children, one grandchild.* He examines my knees, now redder than blood, and says he will help. I remind him of his father. I thank God for gout.

Memory

"In their big, tight-knit family, Bob Levinson has missed many birthdays, weddings, anniversaries and grandchildren."
—Adam Goldman, Associated Press

Pink Shirts

On Thursdays in Miami I wore pink shirts—
buttoned-down, polo, I didn't care. At first
I got funny looks, but then it caught on
and everyone in the office was a good sport.
Hope says my family, my friends, a sea of pink
with pink candles, pink flames, stand vigil
at the White House with pink signs written
with pink markers: *Bring Bob Home.*
I squeeze my index finger until it turns
purplish pink and hold that finger up
to my temple, a gun. Salute the ceiling.
Hail an imaginary cab. Ask for the check.

Daydream

Son, rent a flashy two-door—
a Mustang or Camaro.
Screw it.
Go for the Corvette
and meet me at the gate.
When I hop in, step on it, and don't ever
look in the rearview. Ignore
the red lights, the honks, the signs.
Go 90 on the highway. Don't stop until
we're pulling up in front of our house—
your mother screeching at you
for driving "like a bat out of hell."
Don't stop until it's real.

Godfather

To pass the time, I replay movies. Some come
easy like the *Godfather* films. That's how
I want to go—like Vito Corleone
eating an orange in a garden
with my grandson playing
hide-and-go-seek. I *am* hidden
and I may die, but when I lie down
for that last time, no family
by my side, no one
will know it's the day to weep;
no one will cover my face,
no one will soothe me to sleep.

Checkmate

We each begin with 16 pieces.
Before the first move, my knee knocks
the table and the chessboard
tumbles. Pawns, rooks and queens clatter
on the linoleum. White and black
stand together and march
down the hall. They are unfazed by the fall.
Lined up again in ranks and files
on the cold worn floor,
the pieces move themselves. Each side
taking its turn. Each side playing toward
its endgame. The white king is in the center
and time has almost run out.

The Bird

The partridge repeats his call. I imagine
scribbling a letter on toilet paper,
and tying it to the bird's leg with a cherry stem.
Then it flutters away to deliver that note
to you. You're sitting on the patio
watching the sunset, listening for the mockingbird
that trills and whistles, as my bird flits to the fence.
It pecks its leg free of the stamp-sized package
it has carried across thousands of miles,
and our grandson catches it and runs the note to you.
As it unfolds, you know. You do not have to read
the words to know.

Water

When you see the glare
of plastic litter in the tide,
it's my message in a bottle—
words scrawled on a torn book cover,
ink blurred by water.
When you see the flash
of silver in a wave, it's me
gasping for breath in the ocean
as the water pulls me under.
I'm reaching for you.
Can you see my fingers
just above the blue?

"...for my sighs are many, and my heart is faint."

Lamentations 1:22

Time

Eventually you give up on what if's and why's
and find yourself resigned to fate.
Somewhere a calendar had March 9th
circled. A clock ticked down
the hours, the minutes, the seconds.
Now the hands don't move. That 2007 calendar
has been tossed. Time does not stop,
time does not slow and 3,645 days
have passed since I last saw my wife's face.

Lebanon Hostage Crisis

In the 80s hostages were traded for arms. One life for hundreds of anti-tank missiles. One life for spare parts. One life for anti-aircraft missiles. Dozens of captives held to guard against retaliation, to protest an invasion, to free an imprisoned brother. So, I ask the men, what do you want? Weapons? Money? Insurance? The light is turned out. A crust of bread is thrown to the corner where I cannot reach. The chain anchored to the wall grows shorter. Will the president pay the ransom for my release? Reagan wanted those Americans home. Does anyone want me free? Those Americans were taken. I was taken. Same story. I try to remember: how long were they held? Weren't some of them killed?

Chandra Levy

The news story caught my attention, perhaps because of the last name, perhaps because with long dark hair she reminded me of my daughters, and I along with the rest of the country were left asking that summer: *what happened to Chandra?* I hoped she had run off with thousands of dollars (a payoff from her congressman boyfriend) to live in a gorgeous Bahamas resort. When her remains were found a year later, the family held a memorial, still not knowing who took her. I wonder what my family thinks— am I alive or dead? Should they hold a service? I want to give them closure. To imagine my wife standing at our front window watching the driveway, keeping her phone next to her bed every night, jumping every time one of my colleagues calls to check in, is torture. Why do men capture people, stealing them, locking them away for years or killing them in an instant—a few seconds that ripple through an entire family, an entire city, an entire nation? Chandra is at rest. I want to be at rest.

I Want to Tell You

Call the kids, email our friends, order the banner, bake the cake, blow up the balloons, crank up the music, get out the glassware, open the front door—I'm coming home. See that airplane circling the field—I'm in first class with a full belly of filet mignon and Diet Coke. See that black sedan coming down the hill—I'm speeding.

Wearing a suit, flashing a grin, I run from the car to you—you wearing a long blue dress billowing in the wind with your dark hair streaming behind and when I hug you, kiss you, Iran fades away like a nightmare I can barely recall by lunchtime. Smile for the cameras. Press your hand into mine. Dance with me all night under Florida starlight.

September 11th

These men rebuild the stage of ground zero—
dust-covered papers littered the sidewalks,
the police cars and ambulances crawled by.

        The flash of the camera blinds
        me while I stand blindfold-free
        awaiting rescue or insanity
        to carry me away.

One can only imagine the difficulty
the men had to overcome to create
this basement apartment
from that day's debris.

Yet the men did—glass shards into chains,
broken beams into iron bars,
a bowl and spoon molded from a fallen lamppost,
a faded blanket woven from manila
folders that floated down to the street
as if they contained letters from above.

        What would my letter say? Friends, take this letter
        opener, unfold the page. What does it say?

The men have erased the words
so now you don't have a letter to read.

        All goes black and I'm trapped
        in another airless cage.

Every flashlight beam glaring at me
was torn from a New York City ambulance.
Every beat from a song blaring in the other room
is a footstep—thousands exited the stage.
Every punch to my head, energy
transplanted from an EMT who performed CPR.

One can only imagine the difficulty
for the men to rebuild
terror from terror. My fear
transformed from that of a nation.

I kneel, head covered, hands shackled,
as they fight—who will hold the hammer,
who will saw the wood, who will move
the ladder from one side to the other.

> I want to ask the men why.
> Can they tell me why?

This grief constructs
a ground zero in my chest.

My America

The stars are my name;
this stripe, the Florida state line;
the blue, my veins;
the red, my blood-shot eyes;
the white, the flashes
of pain as I'm struck from behind.
The flag flies high today
and it's me waving goodbye.

"Speak out on behalf of the voiceless and for the rights of all who are vulnerable."

Psalm 31:8

The Haunted House—October 2014

I squeeze my husband's hand as I follow his black coat around dark corners. Cobwebs stick to my hair, middle-schoolers push my back, *hurry, hurry*, the floor slants up and we stumble, catch ourselves against plastic axes, skeletons, giant wire spiders. Hallways lead to rooms—one, with a grown woman in pigtails cradling a decapitated baby doll, dozens of doll heads hang from the ceiling. Another room, a butcher in a blood-spattered apron cuts the air with a cleaver, rubber intestines ooze on the counter. Down the hall, carnival music squeals as a demented clown chases us to the stairs that lead to another scene. The man in an orange jump suit shackled to the wall, his white hair and beard covered in dirt, moans. I think of you. An actor dressed in black approaches the prisoner, screams in his face, wielding a chainsaw. The white beard hangs his head in despair. I have to look away. *We paid to enter this place.*

Dear Bob,

When I call my daughter's name "Leven" and she runs with her long golden hair and her dark brown eyes down the stairs to hug me hello, I imagine you calling your sons' and daughters' names wherever you are now. My children have heard your story and they ask, "Why won't they let him go?"

Before Thanksgiving dinner, we bow our heads and ask God for your release. Later, Leven draws a picture and asks me to send it to you. Where are you? Stone walls or barbed wire fence or a windowless bedroom—I don't tell her that. Instead, I weave a story and point to the drawing. Bob, you're there with that pretty rainbow. You're there with the grass and purple and pink flowers. You're there with the blue clouds and giant butterflies.

Someday I will meet you. After you've hugged all your loved ones, after you've kissed all your grandbabies, after you've had lunch with all your old buddies, after the homecoming parties are finished, after the reporters leave, after the cameras stop flashing, I will deliver my words and my daughter's picture to you. I will tell you how lucky you are to have such a dedicated family. I will wish you the best.

Sincerely,
Catharine

I First Heard Your Name on the Radio

and I couldn't stop thinking of you. Then I read about your family, your life before, and wanted everyone to know of you. When I worry about taxes, my ex-husband, my boss, I look to the ceiling remember Levinson. At a writing conference, I carry your photo, share your plight with the audience, to anyone who will listen *Levinson Levinson.*

A well-dressed man from Chicago tells me he has never heard of you and the shock burns my throat. When a former Marine stops me in the lobby to tell me he knows your story, we speak your name *Levinson Levinson.*

I am a rudderless ship chugging in the night *Levinson Levinson Levinson.*

Water pulls away. The stars hide. All of this for a man I have never met. A man I might have passed in the street without a greeting. Yet I cannot turn or be quiet. I print out your photo, tape it to my bedroom wall, glance your way every morning as I leave the room, and every evening before I turn out the light.

"We will not give up. We know the time is right to act. We humbly ask Iran to deliver on their promise by helping bring my father home. It's their move now."

—Sarah Moriarty, Bob Levinson's daughter

Resources

Anderson, Terry. "Den of Lions: Memoir of Seven Years." Crown Publishing. 1993.

Gudjonsson, Gisli. "The Psychology of Interrogations, Confessions and Testimony:" Wiley. 1992.

Meier, Barry. "Missing Man: The American Spy Who Vanished in Iran." Farrar, Straus, and Giroux. 2016.

Murphy, Major P.J. "Hostage Survival Skills for CF Personnel." http://www.nato.int/docu/colloq/w970707/p6.pdf

Sutherland, Tom. "At Your Own Risk." Fulcrum Publishing. 1997.

Cat Dixon is the author of *Eva* and *Too Heavy to Carry* (Stephen F. Austin University Press, 2016, 2014) and *Our End Has Brought the Spring* (Finishing Line Press, 2015). She is the managing editor of The Backwaters Press, a nonprofit press in Omaha. She is the editor of *Watching the Perseids: The Backwaters Press Twentieth Anniversary Anthology* (BWP, 2017). Her poetry and reviews have appeared in numerous journals and anthologies including *Sugar House Review, Midwest Quarterly Review, Coe Review, Eclectica,* and *Mid-American Review.*

CPSIA information can be obtained
at www.ICGtesting.com
Printed in the USA
LVHW08s2002150718
583869LV00001B/43/P